Dialogues with Rising Tides

Dialogues with Rising Tides

Kelli Russell Agodon

Copper Canyon Press
Port Townsend, Washington

Cover art: René Maltête, *La bouée.* copyright René Maltête/Gamma-Rapho.

Copper Canyon Press is in residence at Fort Worden State Park
in Port Townsend, Washington, under the auspices of Centrum.
Centrum is a gathering place for artists and creative thinkers
from around the world, students of all ages and backgrounds,
and audiences seeking extraordinary cultural enrichment.

LIBRARY OF CONGRESS CATALOGING-IN-PUBLICATION DATA
Names: Agodon, Kelli Russell, author.
Title: Dialogues with rising tides / Kelli Russell Agodon.
Description: Port Townsend, Washington : Copper Canyon Press, [2021] |
    Summary: "A collection of poems by Kelli Russell Agodon"
        —Provided by publisher.
Identifiers: LCCN 2020047969 | ISBN 9781556596155 (paperback)
Subjects: LCGFT: Poetry.
Classification: LCC PS3601.G64 D53 2021 | DDC 811/.6—dc23
LC record available at https://lccn.loc.gov/2020047969

98765432 FIRST PRINTING

COPPER CANYON PRESS
Post Office Box 271
Port Townsend, Washington 98368
www.coppercanyonpress.org

Acknowledgments

Many thanks to the editors, staff, and directors of the following journals, anthologies, and films in which these poems appeared, sometimes in slightly different versions:

Academy of American Poets Poem-a-Day: "Hunger," "Magpies Recognize Themselves in the Mirror"

Alaska Quarterly Review: "At a Cocktail Party, I Am Given a Drink Called *Life Is Fleeting and the Olive Is Short-Lived*"

The American Poetry Review: "Perhaps If We Understood Desire"

B O D Y: "Waltz with Gatsby at 3 a.m."

Cascadia: "Gala Melancholia"

The Cortland Review: "Near-Death Experience"

F(r)iction: "Facedown"

Glass: A Journal of Poetry: "I Don't Own Anxiety, but I Borrow It Regularly," "SOS" (reprinted in *Rewilding: Poems for the Environment*)

Green Mountains Review: "Hold Still"

The Los Angeles Review: "Queen Me"

Meridian: "After Discovering My Husband Bought a Handgun"

Narrative: "Americano," "At the End, We Mistook *Savor* for *Savior,*" "To Have and Have Not," "We Could Go On Indefinitely Being Swept Off Our Feet," "Wintercearig Waltz"

The Nation: "Everyone Is Acting as If We're Not Temporary, and I Am Falling Apart in the Privacy of My Own Home"

New England Review: "Braided Between the Broken"

The Night Heron Barks: "Lightvessel"

One: "Love Waltz with Fireworks"

Orion: "What I Call Erosion"

Pedestal Magazine: "When my therapist tells me
my father's trauma has been transferred to me, I think"

Pine Hills Review: "One Day I'd Like to Live in a World
without Alarm Clocks"

Pittsburgh Poetry Review: "Whiskey-Sour-of-the-Nipple Story"
(reprinted in *Nasty Women Poets: An Unapologetic Anthology of
Subversive Verse*)

Ploughshares: "When Someone Dies, the Sky Whispers *Never
Fall in Love*"

Poetry Society of America: "At Times My Body Leans toward Loss"
(winner of the Lyric Poetry Award judged by Ilya Kaminsky)

PoetsArtists: "Lining Up the Bones," "Thank You for Saving Me,
Someday I'll Save You Too" (winner of Editor's Choice Award)

Redactions: "Modern Love with Absinthe"

Rise Up Review: "The world owes me"

The Shore: "Torn (Old Fabric)"

Tinderbox: "Getting an IUD on the Day of 45's Inauguration"

Valparaiso Poetry Review: "Unsustainable"

Visible Poetry Project: "I Don't Own Anxiety, but I Borrow It
Regularly" (film by Marie Craven), "Love Waltz with Fireworks" (film
by Sarah Durn)

Waxwing: "How Damage Can Lead to Poetry," "Hunter's Moon,"
"String Theory Relationships"

Whale Road Review: "The Sun Doesn't Know It's a Star"

I am deeply grateful for the beacons of light in this world and all who have
supported me through this book and this journey—

A million and more thanks to the hard work, creative brilliance, and
generosity of Michael Wiegers, Elaina Ellis, John Pierce, David Cali-
giuri, Alison Lockhart, Janeen Armstrong, George Knotek, Heidi Sewall,

Joseph Bednarik, Emily Grise, Laura Buccieri, and all Copper Canyon Press for their support of my work. I am so grateful that Copper Canyon Press is in the world—there is no place I'd rather be.

Gratitude and love to my circle of poets: Elizabeth Austen, Michele Bombardier, Ronda Broatch, Jeannine Hall Gailey, Holly J. Hughes, Nancy Pagh, Susan Rich, Marty Silano, Annette Spaulding-Convy, and Melissa Studdard.

Thank you to my poetry sisters & brothers who continue to support & inspire me—Rick Barot, Nancy Canyon, Victoria Chang, Jennifer Culkin, John Davis, Lee Herrick, Ilya Kaminsky, Jenifer Lawrence, Natasha Moni, Aimee Nezhukumatathil, January Gill O'Neil, Dean Rader, Katrina Roberts, Stan Rubin, Diane Seuss, Maggie Smith, Angie Vohries, and all the lights in the poetry community who have been there for me. Thank you to the decades of women from Poets on the Coast and to my family: Susie, Martha, Janice, Jenn & Monty, Kari & Danny, Kim & Matt, Lisa, Suzanne, Stacy, Emilie, Deborah, Camis, Todd, and Rosario.

Special thanks to the Artist Trust, Kathy Cowell at the University of Washington's Whiteley Center, Michelle Hagewood and the Centrum Artist Residency Program, and Michael Tomlinson for being a lifeline while on residency.

All my love and appreciation to Rose, Laney & Gloria—you have been my lightvessels.

And in memory of my three dads: Gale A. Russell, Bert O. Baker, and Dale Cramer, and my nana, Alice J. Mason (1912–2019).

For my mum, Gloria Russell-Baker,
my light in every storm

You have come to the shore.
There are no instructions.

Denise Levertov

CONTENTS

CROSS RIP

Hunger   5

String Theory Relationships   6

Magpies Recognize Themselves in the Mirror   8

Braided Between the Broken   9

Unsustainable   11

I Don't Own Anxiety, but I Borrow It Regularly   12

Whiskey-Sour-of-the-Nipple Story   13

BREAKSEA

Everyone Is Acting as If We're Not Temporary, and
I Am Falling Apart in the Privacy of My Own Home   17

When my therapist tells me my father's
trauma has been transferred to me, I think   18

Waltz with Gatsby at 3 a.m.   19

Lining Up the Bones   20

Lightvessel   21

Bravery   22

SCARWEATHER

At Times My Body Leans toward Loss   25

How Damage Can Lead to Poetry   26

At a Cocktail Party, I Am Given a Drink
Called *Life Is Fleeting and the Olive Is Short-Lived*   28

To Have and Have Not   30

Hold Still   32

The Ocean Is Overflowing   34

One Day I'd Like to Live in a World without Alarm Clocks   35

BLACK DEEP

Hunter's Moon   39

After Discovering My Husband Bought a Handgun   40

Wound Is a Form of Wind   41

Wintercearig Waltz   43

Hesitation Waltz   45

When Someone Dies, the Sky Whispers *Never Fall in Love*   47

Till Death Shatters the Fabulous Stars   48

OVERFALLS

Perhaps If We Understood Desire   51

Love Waltz with Fireworks   52

Modern Love with Absinthe   54

To Help with Climate Change, We Buy Rechargeable Sex Toys   55

The Sun Doesn't Know It's a Star   56

Grace   58

At the End, We Mistook *Savor* for *Savior*   59

SHAMBLES

Getting an IUD on the Day of 45's Inauguration   63

Facedown   64

Torn (Old Fabric)   65

Queen Me   66

Americanitis   67

Unsinkable   68

Americano   70

Heartland   71

SOS   73

Relief

How to Live in a State of Fire   77

Near-Death Experience   78

If I Had to Live Again   79

The world owes me   80

What I Call Erosion   81

Gala Melancholia   82

We Could Go On Indefinitely Being Swept Off Our Feet   83

Thank You for Saving Me, Someday I'll Save You Too   85

Notes   87

About the Author   89

Dialogues with Rising Tides

 Cross Rip

HUNGER

If we never have enough love, we have more than most.
We have lost dogs in the neighborhood and wild coyotes,
and sometimes we can't tell them apart. Sometimes
we don't want to. Once I brought home a coyote and told
my lover that we had a new pet. Until it ate our chickens.
Until it ate our chickens, our ducks, and our cat. Sometimes
we make mistakes and call them coincidences. We hold open
the door then wonder how the stranger ended up in our home.
There is a woman on our block who thinks she is feeding bunnies,
but they are large rats without tails. Remember the farmer's wife?
Remember the carving knife? We are all trying to change
what we fear into something beautiful. But even rats need to eat.
Even rats and coyotes, and the bones on the trail could be the bones
on our plates. I ordered Cornish hen. I ordered duck. Sometimes
love hurts. Sometimes the lost dog doesn't need to be found.

String Theory Relationships

The essential idea is this—the man you love is connected to you
no matter what, but he's also connected to the woman

      down the street with the small dog that barks at the lilacs,
      and she's connected to the cashier at the market who's a bit rough

with your grapes, but he thinks you're ten years younger than you are
and he gives you free saltwater taffy while calling you

      darling—but he also calls her darling, and her dog
      darling, and the man you love along with the grapes.

The essential idea is this—all objects are composed of vibrating anxieties
—everyone wants a window or aisle seat and no one wants to sit

      in the middle. Call it deniability. Call it the flashlight you keep
      by the door never works in emergencies. We are all connected

by the blast that brought us here, the big bang,
the slam dunk, the heavy petting. We can't always be pretty.

      We can't always be the eyelash and the wink, sometimes
      we have to be the ear, sometimes the mouth. You are

and are not the speaker in this story—you are the bridge connected
to the land connected to the man you love and the woman you dislike

      who teaches spin class. It's not personal. It's not personal
      when the universe says it's complicated and you have ten minutes

to understand quantum physics. When the man you love says
there's a new connection called supersymmetry and it exists

      between two fundamentally different types of particles called bosons
      and fermions, you hear *bosoms* and *females*. You hear he's thinking

about the spin teacher with the nice breasts and burrow deeper.
The essential idea is this—someone will always bruise your grapes

      and someone will end up in the middle. Someone you love will break
      your favorite coffee mug and bring you lilacs. And you will be

connected to people who make your eyes roll. You'll be connected
to others who stand on the bridge and consider jumping off. You'll try

      to care for them. And you will not look your age, but you will
      feel sad when you look in the mirror because we all want to live

a little longer, because the dog will die and the cashier has lost his job
for stealing saltwater taffy from the bin, but he still calls you

      darling, calls everyone darling, and today,
      darling, darling, darling, the flashlight works.

Magpies Recognize Themselves in the Mirror

The evening sounds like a murder
of magpies and we're replacing our cabinet knobs
because we can't change the world but we can
change our hardware. America breaks my heart
some days and some days it breaks itself in two.
I watched a woman having a breakdown
in the mall today, and when the security guard
tried to help her, what I felt was all of us
peeking from her purse as she threw it
across the floor into Forever 21. And yes,
the walls felt like another way to hold us
and when she finally stopped crying
I heard her say to the fluorescent lighting,
Some days the sky is too bright. And like that
we were her flock in our black coats
and white sweaters, some of us reaching
our wings to her and some of us flying away.

BRAIDED BETWEEN THE BROKEN

Today apologies were falling
    from the trees and the apples
        were being ignored.

There's a chapter in our lives
    where we tried to shred pages,
        where we tried to rewrite the tale.
Let's call that chapter The Numbness,
    or The Boredom, or the place where we forgot
we were alive.

That morning I woke up and wandered outside
    onto the backtrail,
past the No Trespassing sign into the arms
    of an evergreen or a black bear. It didn't matter
        who held me then; I was the moss, the lichen,
the mushroom growing on the fallen log.

No one expects perfection, except when they do,
    which is always.

    Even you, king of the quiet,
crash when I talk about my brokenness.
    Cover up, your fractures are showing.

In my life I try to apologize for things I haven't done
    yet. Those are the bruised apples of me,
        the possible fruit rotting in the field.

Remember when I kept replaying melancholy?
Remember when I opened our melody with a switchblade?

Rip out the carpet. Mow down the dahlias.
Let's ruin our lives . . .

It felt good to hurt then—
        until it didn't, until we were left
                with bad flooring, a garden
where nothing grew.

You're asking about the next chapter
        and the one after that. You're asking
                what time I'll be home and handing me
a cloth to buff my halo.

Let's put a comma here.
Let's put in a semicolon and think about
        the next sentence.

I dream of erasers. I dream of wite-out.
        I dream of the song where the pharmacist
doesn't judge me for not being able to make it through
the day without some sort of pill.

Unsustainable

When you broke my recycle bin, I
started calling you Fresh Kills.

I want to keep you in my plastic
Happy Meal heart, but what snaps open

stays on Earth forever, my center floating
down a canal until it's swallowed by a seal.

Who cares our plastic drifts as a tagalong
to the sunset, an autobiography of artificial,

a dead whale washed up in the Philippines,
eighty-eight pounds of plastic in its gut?

Damn the turtles! Customers at McDonald's
want their straws! And we could be practical

lovers if we remembered to bring
our reusable totes into the store—you said

the cashier gave me the stink eye for forgetting,
but I was lost in my own head thinking

about my grandmother in hospice, leaving
the store with a casket of even more plastic bags.

It hurts to say my convenience is more important
than the sea. I write a postcard to Earth

—I love you, but watch me navigate your landfills
in stilettos, let me kill your buzz. And you know

I'm talking about the bees now. My hands in the dirt—
if you want to gather honey, don't kick over every hive.

I Don't Own Anxiety, but I Borrow It Regularly

Once I believed the saint I carried could keep me
        safe. He lived in a rain jacket I wore
                to keep out the weather and by weather,
I mean danger. Tell me a story
        where no one dies. That story begins in heaven,
                ends in heaven, and includes chapters
on heaven, heaven, and heaven.

It's not really a story but a wish, or a concern.

Sometimes I wonder if there's one moment
        when no one is dying, where we all exist
                on this planet without loss—
but there are too many of us
        doing foolish things, someone is always sipping
                the arsenic, someone is always spinning
a gun. And then

add old age, misfortune, a tree that's leaned too long
        in the forest and a family of five
headed off for a hike.

We cannot predict our tragedies.

We cannot plan a party for the apocalypse
        because friends of the apocalypse know
                the apocalypse always shows up
uninvited with a half-eaten bag of chips.

This is why some of us wake up
        in the middle of the night looking for a saint—
                and maybe your saint is a streetlight
or maybe the sea, or maybe
        it's the moment you walk out the door
                and exist in the darkness,
announce to the heavens that you're still alive.

WHISKEY-SOUR-OF-THE-NIPPLE STORY

Like every forest, I carry a bonfire
        beneath my shirt. And my mattress?
        It's a featherbed of flames.

I'd want to write you a letter about longing,
        but it has so many wishbone moments
        you'd break, I promise. You—

you'd end up crying or cowarding,
        or being part of the crocodile-tear
        audience asking for a refund. Like most

lovers, my heartstone is actually heartbutter,
        a heart murmur made of wax and it melts,
        it smolders, the way the moth

isn't suspicious of a lighter
        until it moves too close to the fire.
        This is my danger—

I kiss the whalebone without wondering
        what happened to the whale.
        It's inexperience watching

the mercury drip onto my tongue—
        seeing only the beauty of silver,
        not the poison of a perfect teardrop,

like him. Or her. And still.
        Let's not be the part of the drink
        that melts into something weaker.

Like any darling, I trust too much.
        Even a burning building has a purpose,
        as the whiskey does, the nipple, the novel.

So let's begin the story here. Near the plastic
    ocean. Our shirts off. Our drinks filled.
    A bowl of cherries. Believing there aren't any.

Wildfires in sight.

Everyone Is Acting as If We're Not Temporary, and I Am Falling Apart in the Privacy of My Own Home

When he says, *Sometimes we learn the most from losing,*
I think how often I've been bamboozled
by life, how I've dropped a quarter in a slot machine
and instead of cherries got coffins. *Got death?*
       Yeah, I've seen the grim reaper wander
my neighborhood in a Chanel suit with a diamond-
studded scythe because we all want to be overdressed
for the afterlife, we all want to believe
there is a special place for us. But when I watched
the body of my nana fade into thinness I thought,
Please let me leave early—by plane crash, car accident,
lightning bolt—don't let me hold on so long
I am a body longing for someone to text it
—*Hey babe, I'm kind of into you.* To say, *I miss you*
even though I don't visit. Death and we butt-dial
the wrong person. Death on a good drunk
of port.
       I remember my dad once saying,
You are worth more than you think, as I always sold myself
at a discount, and I wish I didn't, I wish I didn't
say how much I hurt on social media
but sometimes I just want to believe I'm not alone
like how we're all doing cartwheels on life's grass
until someone lands in a sinkhole, until one of us
decides it's late and the streetlights
are telling us it's time to return back home.

WHEN MY THERAPIST TELLS ME MY FATHER'S TRAUMA HAS BEEN TRANSFERRED TO ME, I THINK

how long he has been missing
        from the planet, still part of the seawater
                his ashes move through the Pacific
and as she talks, I think of how the sky
        never lets me down—when I look up,
                there is always a cloud to study,
a new shade of blue. How lucky I am
        to see the moon rise like a bull's-eye
                over the Cascades—someone
has shot a hole through the entire universe,
        and I wonder who held the gun,
                how we arrive at places
we want to leave from.
        She tells me the reason I wake up
                screaming is because
no one ever dealt with that pain and now
        I wear it like a silver blanket
                and each night I wrap myself
in suffering instead of sheets—*It's what you carry,*
        what you will pass on—and when she says,
                There are ways to get through this,
I think about how much I like the roasted corn
        salsa I make on weekends, how the shallots
                and cilantro give it just enough bite
and the lime juice reminds me how once
        in Mexico, after I lost my wedding ring,
                I did a body shot off a woman
I didn't know and how sticky she was
        and how the tequila made the night a little quieter
                and the stars made the beach feel like a church,
a celebration, and when I stumbled across the sand
        I learned to love the sand, even when I couldn't
                move from it, even when its coldness wrapped
around my skin, even when I almost fell asleep.

Waltz with Gatsby at 3 a.m.

If only sleep could help me
        sweep up the confetti on the staircase,
        or what it really is—shredded

cabbage on the kitchen porch.
        There's an old dog limping in the yard
        and he's my old dog. Bless the sweet

fog he roams through and call that sweet fog
        God, or grass, or indeterminate years.
        In the physical world, we are just bodies

losing our structure, my composition
        from breadstick to cinnamon loaf,
        honeycomb to just the drip of honey.

Gatsby has changed from dog
        in the waves, dog in the field, to dog
        needing help when his back legs don't hold.

We're all trying, my dog slowly
        returning to the bluesmoke
        he came from, while I chop

cabbage and watch the moon
        begin its slow circle into another
        time zone. In my head, I am Zelda

and this is my party, but the truth is
        it's almost morning, truth is
        I'm the worker bee and not the queen.

LINING UP THE BONES

Life. Is dominoes. Is a phone call at 2 a.m., 3 a.m., who has died,
who is, who may be
            dying. Father in a blue cup, set atop
a plate we hope won't. Break. Who is breaking? Who broke
the blue cup, the pickup truck veering off the edge
of a calendar
            year.   Is pill bottles. Is orchids. Empty
beer cans tossed behind a parachute. Is rifle. Is possible
death, dying, or accident. A wildfire, grease fire, but
the turkey dinner survives, meaning—good enough
for us. Meaning the feathers were. Plucked.
The pumpkin pie never bought.
When the dead call.
            Laughter is the new sorrow. Is heart
attack, is hard
-boiled eggs. No. Only shells. Like bullets. Broken,
but from a distance. A cherub. Lost. Like a ring.
Who glued us together? A marble, a crystal ball
contains both—
            fear and future. A foreshadowing. Two women
holding hands as they walk to a funeral. Are bottle heavy.
Are both. Griefheavy. One leans like a domino.
Don't let her. Fall. Breaksea.
            In a blue cup
of shadow. Leaves underneath. Your mother will always hold you
up. Cat's-eye. Continue on. A photograph
of an escape hatch in her pocket.

Lightvessel

Tonight under an unkissed moon—
the recipe is disappearing, a dialogue
with rising tides and a lightship
crashing against a blue shore of healing.
When I struggle in a diorama

> of traffic, I become the silver orb
> in a city's pinball machine—*be here now*
> —flung against the pulsing lights
> and hectic newspapers that papier-mâché
> themselves to my legs, my life, I forget

it's been years since I've seen neon
flicker, now the only language I speak
is seascape, a searchlight, a map
made of unintelligible emotions
I try to navigate. If I could be any age,

> I'd be the heartbeat just before
> the butter melts, where everything
> is soft and easy, a cookbook
> for a sacred life. And when I'm desperate
> for spices, I go to the bodega to buy love,

but the owner gives me wine and a new pen,
says, *This is probably better*—and how can I
argue? I've forgotten to pack a lunch,
forgotten how much I ache for anyone
to rest their words against my lips.

BRAVERY

is what I hold as I cry
    in the shower, water spiraling
    down my skin as if my body
is a bell curve and crisis exists
    between breast and belly,
    an empty ache behind a ribcage,
a daughter in a different state.
    Maybe I'm in a state of depression
    or maybe it's another exhausted evening
where I am turning the knob
    of the shower and the woman
    stepping in is lost and searching
for warmth, to taste the salt
    of the ocean just to prove to herself
    she still remembers how to swim,
how to skinny-dip. *Bravery,* I tell
    the body who is now curled
    on the shower floor, her hair
a New Year's resolution of rainfall,
    her mascara a river of ink down her
    cheekbones, and when I pull her
from drowning, I think about how easy it is
    to be anonymous in your own home,
    how I will wrap a blue robe around her
damp body and lead her to the bed,
    undress her, dry her face, and I will
    close the blinds on the windows
so what the world sees will not be the woman
    with wet hair on the blue pillow,
    but the dream I give her where blessings
are her backdrop and her weapon is waking up—
    Bravery, say the morning birds outside her
    window, bravery, as I watch her rise.

 Scarweather

AT TIMES MY BODY LEANS TOWARD LOSS

You didn't remember seeing the deer give birth
on the highway, so when I said, *I worry about things
I can't control,* you told me the pitchfork I carry
in my mind stabs inward,
          like the day was sun-filled but what I saw
was how I bumped the planter of gerbera daisies
and the moth fluttered up into the beak of a bird.
Death and dinner. A minor accident and something dies.
Like the woman who drove to work crying in her car—
when I saw her, she waved, a reflection in the glass,
the good fortune of having a job to drive to, but the collision
of sadness in the left ventricle of her heart. Who can hold
a knife without thinking for just a second, which vein
          is most useful
to slice into? *Most everyone,* you say
as you dull down the ends of my pitchfork, *most everyone,*
you say as you unlock the door to our home.

How Damage Can Lead to Poetry

It's morning and there's a poem in my jacket
    pocket, and I like how that sounds:
jacket pocket,

but I'm thinking about what the stranger penciled
    in my book, how he circled the word
mistakes, then wrote, *How damage can lead
to poetry.*

    We are quiet birds under the morning
glory—*jacket pocket*—in the near-heart of the dying
hydrangeas. Damage creates the thought
    of brokenness: my ocean never has enough
        songbirds, my life never has enough

song. It's morning and there's a whisper in my family
    history—I know the suicides, the stories
        of strange deaths: brother choking
on a balloon, sister tripping on the church steps
        and hitting her head so perfectly

her arteries became a celebration, Bastille Day,
    New Year's Eve. And she was. And he was. Gone.

Even though I wasn't there, I still see my sisters
    finding our father's first wife in the greenhouse
where he grew orchids—*jacket pocket*
—a gunshot to her head.

This is postpartum with suicide corsages—
    psychopsis, dendrobium—a landscape
of the dying, a three-year-old finding
    her mother, blood on the leaves

of the plants nearby. My sister would later say,
It's why I dislike the colors of Christmas,
     and yet, she. And yet, she. Grew up
like so many of us, near-heart, fingers
       in the roots of the dying, and mostly,
       somewhat, okay.

At a Cocktail Party, I Am Given a Drink Called *Life Is Fleeting and the Olive Is Short-Lived*

The horizon is a body leaning backward
and as she laughs the moon becomes an olive,

slips down her cleavage, slips down
the front of her dress . . . Wait.

Sometimes I stumble over the clover,
the cleaver, stumble over the live and downer,

the lover and leaver, sometimes, it's a tumble
over the horizontal misunderstanding

of lying down in a bed of pleasure, leisure,
a bed of please and release, of sure, and plea,

and maybe some ease here. Sometimes
we tap dance over the harder spots, the spaces

on our spine where we'd rather waltz,
we'd rather fall backward into the sea,

but instead we gather. I keep silent
about the fear of all of us not making it

through the day, keep silent about all that love,
all I want to touch or not touch,

all those sailings into an evening of icebergs.
Sometimes I'm afraid when our bodies fall

backward, our hearts will quit and we'll be left
with only sunsets. Because tomorrow

may never come. Because tomorrow
is coming but you don't want it to, because

we ache for a few more days and
our only guarantee is made of dust.

To Have and Have Not

As a child I believed suicide only happened
to the Hemingways.

But it's more like Clue—
my grandfather in the VA hospital
with a shotgun.

Wait, he's not the murderer!

Ah, but he murdered himself—
so he is! Don't let the game derail you:
        winner take nothing, winner take all.

For a long time, I never knew taking one's life
was a major our family excelled at.

A degree in suicide? We swallowed it, reloaded,
a master's degree in dying.

Once a cousin said: We're just like the Hemingways,
but not as rich. Though sometimes death happens

in beautiful spaces. It's Clue again,
but this time in the orchid room, a mother
with a handgun in her purse.

She forgot to leave a note,
but remembered to fold the clothing
at the end of her daughter's bed.

It's 3 a.m., do you know where your suicidal wife is?
Plot twist—she killed herself in the daylight,
while her daughters were taking a nap.

Families are noteworthy through madness—

> the American dream when it becomes a nightmare,
> their only drawback the mess they leave
> for relatives to clean up.

But we are not the Hemingways—I say as I slip

an orchid behind my ear—
we scrub the blood away, untie the noose,
we keep on caring for our ghosts.

HOLD STILL

There wasn't enough
ethyl acetate in the killing jar
and the butterfly awoke
halfway through the process.

It's a falsehood to believe we can pin life
to our walls.

Fact: the child was crying.
Fact: the parents' fingers were covered in orange dust.

This is both science and a hobby.
The childrearing, not the pinning
of a butterfly. Believing insects

should be on our walls is a minor deception
of beauty, of art.

Once on a road trip from Friendship to Oblivion
you asked me if I'd pull the wings
off a butterfly for a million dollars. I said no.

I said no, not because I wasn't ravenous
for money, but because I've never been
interested in mishandling any life but my own.

You told me I should and was wrong
for saying no, said, *You could donate the money
to butterfly research, buy butterfly farms.*

While I doubted butterfly farms existed,
the research made sense, still

I told you it comes down to choice,
one person deciding what's best for everyone.

You shook your head and asked me a similar question
about pulling the legs off spiders—
One million dollars, you said

—believing that we choose who we hurt
based on their beauty, because the things that frighten us
are easier to kill.

The Ocean Is Overflowing

Maybe it's how the waves feel. Like tongue.
Maybe you'll pamper my taste. For tragedy.

How disaster is a distance. I'll drive to.
How I want. What's overflowing. In my lungs.

I want to be saltlicked. An artificial mermaid.
In Birkenstocks. And tie-dye. Unaware

what year it is. Who is president. Who wants
to be. President. Like the summers I spent.

On a beach blanket. In Unemployment Lane.
As they called it. The place where all of us.

With too much. Time. And not enough. Money.
Spent the day. God how much. I miss

secondhand smoke. Not knowing
what could kill. Us. What we shouldn't suck.

Into our lungs. And like the ocean. I want to rest.
Here. A past world of the casually uninformed.

Where I didn't. Need much. Maybe. Enough
money. For noodles. Maybe a bent book. A little

baby. Oil. Because we had no idea. What we were.
Supposed to be. Afraid of.

One Day I'd Like to Live in a World without Alarm Clocks

Last night I wrote you a letter between the scars
on your body like sketching light
between what was once pain,
and when I was done, I signed my name
on your thigh—*Autographed Copy,*
I thought, but at this point you were
asleep and dreaming of another artist,
someone's hands on your body,
or maybe, because I heard your stomach
rumble when I was writing my favorite
line about the constellations
of you across your abdomen,
I wondered whether your dream had descended
into our kitchen, to the plate of scrambled eggs
and green onions I left out,
and when you went to grab a napkin,
you realized it was covered in pen marks,
and you wondered how to wipe
your face without a lightning bolt of blue
across your lips, and this is when I love you
most—when you are covered in my smeared
words, and when I fell asleep beside you,
I tried to enter your dream by knocking
on the kitchen window—*Don't wake up,*
I have strawberries I picked from our garden,
I am holding the three stars we always talk about
and they are not even burning my palm.

Black Deep

Hunter's Moon

The first person you fall in love with
will be a deer. You will want to cradle him
but his instinct is to vanish. Scuttle. Scurry.
He may lie down at the end of the forest
in the sorrel, but you won't ever see him
even with the binoculars you bring into the wild.
Perhaps he'll disappear on a trail beside you
and you may be charmed by his departure.
But maybe he is the hunter and you are the deer.
You worry about his heart spear, what he keeps
hidden, because you know you will never be a hunter;
you are just tired of walking through this forest alone.

After Discovering My Husband
Bought a Handgun

I said nothing
as you found a mistress and filled her
with bullets   hid her in the laundry room
when I came home.   How could I know
there was another?   I was aimed
at our future   an anniversary
without bullet wounds.
You're not the first man
to believe betrayal is beautiful.
You promised me nothing
said gun was your new passport
     your new itinerary
said gun is the lock we never had
     on our doors
said, It's a dangerous world now—
     gun will keep us
safe, said gun gives good dead
gun to my head   gun in my bed
gun lets you do things to her
     when she is loaded
said gun is the lover you always wanted
it's always gun   it's always fun
to have a new lover
so I slid my fingers around her thin neck
and pulled hard.

Wound Is a Form of Wind

In the darkness it's impossible
to see the darkness.

How long must you know someone
until they see your scars?

You reach for me and I become
a kite in your diorama, a string,
something you try to hold.

Maybe I'm confused,

wound in a calamity
of bedsheets, sheet music—

leaving, returning, maybe floating
away. The wind harms what is growing
outside the broken window.

In darkness, it's easy to be in a tangle—

my eyes shut, head on the pillow (*kiss me*)
your hand beneath my hip bone (*does this hurt?*)

—does the wind keep telling me to stay?

In darkness, I can't see the flowering
plum tree or trust its branches lowering,

wind: what you do to the string of a kite
wind: what causes the kite to fly

limbs weaken, break off into the yard.

During the storm you said you loved
how I dismantled the bed,
how I was a universe to untangle.

I want to wind myself in a midnight
of stars. My gown is dark matter.
Against the sky, I am invisible, wound
tight—if night is a bruise, so am I.

WINTERCEARIG WALTZ

I add three cups of powdered sugar
        to the angel food cake,
        Made with real angels, I say to the shadows.

The water spider in the measuring cup
        does the backstroke. The snow you shoveled
        in the driveway holds us captive.

I lick my fingers and stroke a blessing
        across my tongue. We are all achieving things
        these days. You ask me if waltzing

should be taught in school instead of physics.
        When I respond, *What doesn't move us forward*
        becomes part of the problem,

we know this is us and the economy.
        I am the snowball
        wishing you were a supernova

and you are a supernova wishing I'd lower
        my expectations. Later, when
        I add gin to the devil's food cake,

the devil removes his muzzle.
        The cat peers into the kitchen
        and sees a ghost, which I am

these days, as well as a devil.
        You and the cat wish I were
        baking pumpkin pie

and we were happier, but my dessert
        is a forgotten dance, a shot
        of something in my drink.

Sometimes after I stop crying, the moon
     places its hands around my hips—
     We're cool, I say and roll over

to my other lover, *pillow,*
     my other lover, *murmur,* my other
     lover—a newly discovered word.

HESITATION WALTZ

The hesitation is this—
       death arrives holding orchids, death
       in a tuxedo, dapper

and carrying a bottle of champagne.
       How do you explain disappearing?
       It's the reason I hate magicians

—what disappears, they can always return.
       When my father died, a spider built a web
       in his prosthetic leg. When my father died,

I spilled orange juice in the ballroom
       just to see if God appeared
       as a waltz across the floor.

How do I stop speaking to the invisible?
       When I heard David Copperfield purchased
       an island the size of London, I hated him more.

It's egotistical to steal so much of the world
       for yourself as well as a classic title for your name.
       The hesitation is maybe I'd want my own island,

maybe I'd be that selfish. Maybe I'd ask for a cocktail
       with a slice of moon. Maybe I'd make people call me
       Charlotte's Web. Maybe Princess Leia.

You know how I always seem to be struggling,
       even when the situation doesn't call for it?
       I'd rather be lukewarm. I'd rather be Luke Skywalker.

The hesitation is when I went to see *Star Wars*
       at a drive-in, I could not tell the difference
       between the movie and the sky. I kept talking

to God at the snack bar. I kept asking for extra
butter, a little more salt. I was young and my wings
glimmered. How do I get that sparkle back?

Maybe now when I look to the moon
I still see the Death Star. Maybe I drink
too many mimosas at baby showers.

The hesitation is all my life I keep waiting.
I hear the music in the background, but see
a lilac field and cemetery of white lilies

in the distance, a catastrophe of orchids.
The hesitation is maybe life is a cobweb,
not an organizational chart.

WHEN SOMEONE DIES, THE SKY WHISPERS
NEVER FALL IN LOVE

Because loss is the back of the photograph
we never look at, I write your deathbed
scenario on the palm of my hand
      while your husband prays
and your mother brings dessert to the funeral.
      So sensitive, I hear you say at the edge
of heaven, the end of history, *So strange*
how we're here for only an eyeflash.
      You stumble with your new angel wings,
and laugh—*All that suffering!* as you dust off
your glimmer—and I walk down a flagstone path
trying to tidy the flowers others left for you,
      as if blossoms were enough to hold
what isn't there anymore, *It's a gesture
of unneeded sympathy a deathdate too late,* you say.
      And I love that your ghost
continues to complain about the living
and writes me love letters in the scent
of jasmine blooming near the window
      *—If you're trying to outrun pain,
that's a race you won't win,* I hear
the rain tell the sidewalk, in the thunder
that almost knocks down the front door.

Till Death Shatters the Fabulous Stars

Open the window and see how the horizon
was drawn with a knife. Three brothers—mountaintops.
Two sisters—volcanoes ready to blow. I'm devoted
to the broken
    clamshells
    climate
    cockleshells
in us. I know I mention the sky too many times
in a day. I know I keep pointing out the same brown bird.
It reminds me of an ashtray my sister made

when children were allowed to make ashtrays
out of clay. My mother put her Carltons in the freezer
because she didn't need them. My smoking father

is in a grave we forgot
    to plant the rosemary
    to mow the grass
    to water the basil
to engrave. I like the songs playing from the nests.
Waxwings don't sing in minor notes, they know happiness
stems from trills, the vibration of berries.

Time is a long sunrise where we wait for our halos.
Night is the ash that covers the light. Lessons
in disappearing. We keep losing
    glaciers
    entire species of birds
    honeybees
ourselves. For the last year I've wanted to undo everything,
unsew the haze from my eyelids—*you are here to be
swallowed up.* Open the window, let the stars burn.

Overfalls

PERHAPS IF WE UNDERSTOOD DESIRE

It's early and I've found   what we love
is sometimes silenced by   what we also love

not because the moon is the problem
but because two moons are   a galaxy
dazzling with fullness
but you can't keep a universe to yourself

sometimes you have to return
a gentle planet to its shelf

not because   you were too greedy
but because   tenderness is not for sale

it's early so I tiptoe through my sins
not because I'm thoughtful of others
sleeping but because I wouldn't mind

living in a world with two moons
I wouldn't mind slipping a few satellites
into my pocket instead of a life
with limited lunar events

tenderness is wholesale and it wants me
to pull it from the shelf   tenderness
has a voice box   tenderness keeps

saying *close your eyes*   *close your eyes*
tenderness will not turn off

Love Waltz with Fireworks

Seventeen minutes ago, I was in love
    with the cashier and a cinnamon pull-apart,
    seven minutes before that, it was a gray-

haired man in argyle socks, a woman
    dancing outside the bakery holding
    a cigarette and a broken umbrella. The rain,

I've fallen in love with it many times,
    the fog, the frost—how it covers the clovers
    —and by clovers I mean lovers.

And now I'm thinking how much I want to rush up
    to the stranger in the plaid wool hat
    and tell him I love his eyes,

all those fireworks, every seventeen minutes, exploding
    in my head—you the baker, you the novelist,
    you the reader, you the homeless man on the corner

with the strong hands—I've thought about you. But
    in this world we've been taught to keep
    our emotions tight, a rubber-band ball where

we worry if one band loosens, the others will begin
    shooting off in so many directions. So we quiet.
    I quiet. I eat my cinnamon bread

in the bakery watching the old man still sitting
    at his table, holding his handkerchief as he drinks
    his small cup of coffee. And I never say,

I think you're beautiful, except in my head,
    except I decide I can't
    live this way. I walk over to him and

place my hand on his shoulder, lean in close
and whisper, *I love your argyle socks,*
and he grabs my hand,

the way a memory holds tight in the smallest
corner. He smiles and says,
I always hope someone will notice.

Modern Love with Absinthe

As I dissolve the sugar cube in my drink,
         there's a comma in the sky,
my hipsway across the beach, your body,
a sign, a sigh: *Lifeguard not on duty.*
                    You and I are close again.
I eat the lemon cake, you do the dishes.
I undress, you
undress me. We are strange tides
         of living, a sentence
of years where half of what I tell you
is true. But we've sipped a marriage on that,
                    the sweet dissolving
in darkness—yes, all that bitterness
is hard to love—but I'm thankful
for the precision of your fingers,
the ability to unfasten me from the lace
of decades holding me in.

TO HELP WITH CLIMATE CHANGE, WE BUY RECHARGEABLE SEX TOYS

When the saleslady says, *This one gets about forty-five minutes*
before needing to be recharged, I joke, *Forty-five minutes?*
What is this, amateur hour? Somewhere in another city
a woman is making a sign for a protest that reads,
The earth is hotter than my imaginary girlfriend.
We're doing our part in different ways like the people
who arrived in a Prius holding a pamphlet, *The Eco-Friendly*
Guide to Sex Toys—they bought the handblown
dildo created by a local artist. As I pick up
the feather tickler from the bargain bin, I think
of the decline of North American birds, three billion birds
missing and how each year fewer cliff swallows return
to our neighborhood. And as I hold the blue vibrator
I was told Oprah recommended (a detail I kind of doubt),
I'm reminded of a sky I saw when I was eight,
before the brown haze of smog turned the city
into a health concern, the wife of a superhero dying
of lung cancer at forty-four even though she never smoked,
the thin layer of ash we wonder about then wipe off
our car windows before we drive home.

The Sun Doesn't Know It's a Star

We live in a world where every season begins
with a bullet exiting a shadow

and someone praying for her lilacs, for her
honeysuckle to take root. It's a hundred degrees

in the shade and the weather argues with itself
over who has the better candidate—

stop, you're both wrong, the sky wins
by a meteor shower. The stars aren't watching

television tonight, they're out waltzing
through modern galaxies, a ballroom

of ghosts where everything is about daybreak
and dazzle, how much moondust will trail

into the house. Somewhere between ego
and starshine, we lost our hatbox of kindness,

maybe we stored it in the back closet because fear
seemed much more dramatic on the living-

room table. And we wonder why we think
our neighbor's a spy and everyone is so on edge.

Some days the stranger planting honeysuckle
to stabilize the cliff leans too far

into the galaxy and we fall
into her optimism. Trust what you don't

know, like the honeybees that rise
from the heart of the canyon, watch them

like small suns circling the slight blossoms,
watch them slide in, knowing

even a small amount of nectar
is a greater sum than none.

GRACE

Even those who are living well
are tired, even the rock star
who swallowed the spotlight,
even the caterpillar asleep
in an unbalanced cocoon.
  Who knows how
to be happy when a lamb
is birthed just to be slaughtered
at a later date?
  It's so tiring
how every day is also a miracle—
the drunk bees in the plum
blossoms, the sliver of sun
through the branches—
  then on an early morning
walk we find the farmer's
granddaughter has fallen
in love with the lamb,
so it will be saved
and named Grace.
  And we are spared,
for a moment, from a new
loss and life frolics
across a field of wildflowers
never knowing all it has escaped.

At the End, We Mistook *Savor* for *Savior*

With your head on my thigh, it's hard to think
        about regret.

The newspaper is a mosaic
        of misfortune and terra-cotta planters
always break despite our placing them
        in spaces we think are safe.

It's not necessary to see forgiveness
        as a lake that will never be filled
but I'm a beginner here, I fill a kiddie pool
        and call it a spa.

Life is lonely
        in the best of times
and what we desire will come back
        to haunt us in run-on sentences.

What we desire will break, be broken.
        What we desire will fall asleep
while we are brushing our teeth
        in the bathroom.

And some will carve loss
        into a vein and call it a tattoo.
And some will serve cake with a side
        of hunger. And we will lick the frosting

from our fingers knowing we're finishing this
        recipe, and we will lick and lick again.

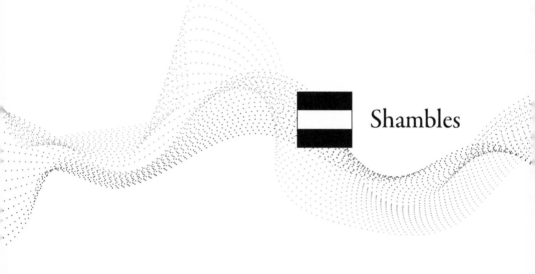

Shambles

GETTING AN IUD ON THE DAY OF 45's INAUGURATION

My body is a flag across the table.
    I am spreading my legs because
        this is what women do. My body
isn't sure it wants to
    carry this, but my body has been bleeding
        for two months, a period of patriotism,
    though my colors run.
        From above, what you see are three women
in a room, two fully clothed, one in a paper
    gown on a table. The one in a paper
        gown is a flag, her feet in metal stirrups.
What she doesn't know is tomorrow.
    What she doesn't know is how many of us
        there are until we all show up.
A woman holds the device to slip inside me,
    to stop the bleeding, to stop the babies,
        to offer the progesterone my body
is refusing to make. My body is a flag woven
    in the metaphysics of bleeding. How to sew
        a perfect woman. How to hem
a menstrual flow. While I wait in my gown,
    the nurse says there may be a little pain,
        for the next four years,
as she comforts—her hand
    on my arm while the doctor inserts
        her hand, a speculum, the device,
inside me. My body is a ragged flag,
    worn but still flying.

FACEDOWN

The man working on my back says,
I'm concerned with your relationship to pain.
He's joking, but not, his elbow bearing
down on some back bedroom in the house
of my spine. He asks how it feels
and I say, *It's a good hurt.* But harder.
Deeper. He presses a star in an upper
galaxy and the heat of an astronomical object
dies in my shoulder blade. He tells me
he can trace the curve of what I'm made of.
I ask him to get under my wingspan,
press deep into the part of me that aches.
Classical music plays in the background
and I remember the violinist who left me
in high school after a friend slid himself
inside me even though I said no.
How can we repair another lifetime?
How can we break away from what we hold?
The man working on my back
moves his thumb slowly down the edges
of my vertebrae, says, *I know we can heal this.*
It doesn't have to hurt to be good.

TORN (OLD FABRIC)

I've begun praying again   because I don't trust
the sand to hold me   or maybe I was born
with stitches on the edges   of my heart
a flimsy doll who thought she   could swim
thought she could fill the ocean   with her tears
maybe the world has wings   and it's what
keeps us floating between   storm surges
or maybe there's a string tied   from the lip
of America to a hook in the ceiling   of a galaxy &
like a disco ball we spin hoping   our mirrors
catch light   like watercolors we   want to mix
we kneel as the anthem begins   we pray   we float
underwater   we praise   we write   our roof is falling
meteors   remember our dandelion   crowns how
beautiful we thought we were when   we painted
our chins with buttercups   lucky child   you loved
this world more when you couldn't see   its tears.

QUEEN ME

Playing chess I realize how tired I am
of the patriarchy, how the winning move
involves the king, the useless piece
who can only skate square to square.
When playing checkers, I taught my daughter
to say as she slides her plastic red chip
the full length of the board: *Queen me.*
It returns to my youth when I wanted
to play baseball and the coach said,
Girls can only play softball and tossed me
what looked like a small leather planet.
Queen me, I wanted to say when I couldn't
be captain of the kickball team, couldn't
play Santa in the school show. *Queen me,*
my daughter says to the neighbor boy,
who without question places another checker
on her piece. Later I hear him say
to my daughter, *Queen me,* as they begin
another game. *Queen me,* he says again
and again as the universe begins to shift
like a tilted tiara finally made right.

AMERICANITIS

There are things now considered antique:
rotary phones, typewriters, sitting in the cabin
of a plane watching night come at us

through an open cockpit door. Who knew
a man would steal our trustfulness? Who knew
we'd find a treasure, a belt, a gun?

Because I was once lost on Tom Sawyer's island,
the worst thing I fear is everything.

Someone will see my raft is made of popsicle sticks,
someone will find my treasure chest of shame.

Today I overheard a conversation in a theater:
     I had to look up if I was an alcoholic.
     I had to take an online test.

When a single white male entered the movie
a half hour late, I whispered to a friend:
I hope he's a masturbator & not a mass shooter.

Because the things I can hold in my hand—
a coin, a constellation—both make me wealthy.
When the aliens land on this planet I will tell them:

     We're rich but we haven't realized it yet.
     We're rich but we're terribly cruel, too.

I drive the highway but not before seeing something
on the side of the road, *A fur coat,* I say.
Someone must have thrown away a fur coat.

Place free-floating anxiety here.
Place tragic occurrence in the white space.

Unsinkable

Usually bad things happen in the conversation
    we're having, in the town we are/aren't
        living in, in my/your head, in person,
standing in front of us with a citation,
    a summons, a bill we can't afford to pay.

Usually bad things name themselves
    Brad, and pin us to the bed or don't
        call, pin us to the bed then smoke a cigarette
while we clean up in the bathroom.
    Usually bad things are right-handed and carry
        too much change in their back pocket.

Like the bad thing that happened
    in your/my household, in your/my youth,
        that friend whose spouse left
for the jogging partner even though
    we all saw it coming, well-mannered
        observers drinking wine with the wolves,
cracking a cork on his/her fang.

Usually bad things happen when a woman keeps
    a suitcase full of handguns and a makeup bag
        of bullets, how she loves to place her lips
around the curve of the barrel,
    slip her tongue against the trigger
        —every few seconds another shooting
star, every few seconds someone is gunnysacked
    into a bridesmaid dress they didn't want to wear.

Usually bad things happen like meteors
    landing on cars, through the roof of a couple
        making love after their toddler is finally asleep.

Or that moment we think we're finished
        and we kiss again, bewildered, be wildfired,
                like those last moments we waltzed
while the ship sank. We're drowning
        in the unknown, searching for shells
                on a beach of rogue waves.

Americano

April is not the cruelest month,
    but the cruelest barista
        who didn't smile back,
who misspelled my name
    and rolled her eyes
        when she thought customers
weren't watching. Coffee is sometimes
    the color of ruin, sometimes dust.
        Sometimes the ferry workers
talk of the worst-case scenarios
    when I'm within earshot.
        It's Homeland Security Day.
It's we-almost-have-enough-life-rafts—
    except for you and you.
        When the boat is on fire,
there's only so much you can do
    even though your reflection
        in the window thinks you can
do more. Underestimate the beauty
    in the world and spill coffee
        down your shirt. The clouds
are heavy as they always are in April,
    the month not the girl,
        but this is not suffering,
it's believing that miracles happen
    to other people. We're adrift
        in the grayness
slipping through the window—
    half the city sees sunrise,
        the other half is lost in fog.

HEARTLAND

You want me to have faith
  but there's a dog under your porch,
a stray dog and he's dying.
  You tell me names of gods I do not recognize
so I can blame them for my insomnia,
  so you can blame them
for the dog who appeared with a limp
  and trembled, who stumbled deep
beneath your deck to hide away.

I'm leaving for somewhere
  because I've never been to Walla Walla
and you are praying for good news,
  as the dog is a simple breath now
next to the food and water you left
  near the stair, next to the leap of cliff
you live by. The topic is not the overhang,
  how far we have to fall, but closer—
how do we live when there is so much
  dying?

The tomatoes are no longer growing
  in the garden, instead their leaves are black.
There was a surprise cremation
  of an evergreen wrapped with ivy
by a man with an ax.
  And everyone knows someone
who is *living with/dying from* cancer
  depending on your optimistic wording.

I am pouring myself a gravestone
  of iced tea and going on a slow ride
down a long highway because everyone
  is trying to keep this dog
alive, and what I can't take is another life

I couldn't save, and honestly,
I've never seen the heartland
        or been to Walla Walla where
the onions are sweet
        and you can drive by farm after farm
not knowing what skeletons
        are buried deep within their fields.

SOS

In a country of too much everything

—too many orcas dying and chemical fires

creating radiant lightning—we wake to a morning

of mourning what didn't live, a woman

stepping onto the train tracks and us,

a block away, hearing the thud.

Sometimes we break the wishbone

without making a wish—my arm on your arm,

my head on your chest as if this will be

our silhouette forever, as if we're in charge

of our own disappearing.

Sometimes we want to cut ourselves

out of the world, but we laugh because

none of our knives are sharp enough

nor our dedication to leaving.

So tonight with the moon wilting, evening

overflowing into the canal where a nuclear sub

passes, guardians of what we can't see,

our reflections are employed by the waves

as if disaster were our business, as if we're not

wildly waving our distress flag

from the edge of this eroding shore.

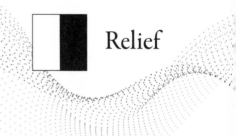

Relief

HOW TO LIVE IN A STATE OF FIRE

Sometimes I look through the other side
of my binoculars to keep the world at a distance.

When the West Coast was on fire, I dreamed
of roasting marshmallows while the smoldering

outside my open window kept me company.
Sometimes I trust too much.

This is where guardian angels come in.
I forget to lock my doors.

Maybe I've given a stranger my keys.
Maybe the bears have my password.

I've never looked up *Are guardian angels real?*
I've never looked up *How to roast marshmallows*

while the world is on fire. Some nights the moon
is a lightship floating in a shallow sea,

so bright I dim the porch light.
Much of my life, I've argued with moths

until I realized moths are guardian angels
who'll be swallowed by sparrows. *Everything needs to eat,*

my daughter says as we watch the Animal Channel,
her hand placed directly over my eyes.

Near-Death Experience

I left heaven because the pillows were filled
with grief and the bedsheets had a thread count

of longing. None of the angels wanted to talk
about moisturizer, my recipe for vegan pizza,

and every morning I'd wake up hoping for sin
with my muesli, but instead they offered me

sugar while the living continued sending
their prayer requests to my mailbox. I decided

I was wrong about desire—that Earth, while messy,
had the best sex and wi-fi. Maybe I was tired

of trying to explain to saints how it was more fun
to be tempted. And how I missed band-aids

and credit cards, apologies and sad songs.
I left heaven with an unmade bed and enough

light to fill a stairway. Maybe in real life the wound
is misrepresented, mismanaged by its handlers;

pain and loss are D-list celebrities we try to avoid,
but in between the aching, maybe sacred is tangled

in the bedsheets, maybe the rip in the pillowcase
is what helps us re-create the clouds.

IF I HAD TO LIVE AGAIN

When someone says the world is mostly water,
I say, *And poets.* And when they tilt their head
in a what-the-fog moment, I've already moved on
to the lower parts of sky, the clouds I form
into halos, the oversimplified gulls
like writers grouped together by wingspan
trying to unearth oyster shooters
from the shells on the beach.
      Maybe America is in romantic decline,
a stock photo we downloaded, what we thought
was happiness—insert sunflower field, insert
favorite brand name, a couple drinking
mochas. I've sipped from that mug, sometimes
I've tasted the burn, sometimes the lukewarm,
and in my mind I hear Roethke saying,
      You'll be happy to know
      today I was only mildly depressed.
And a second nuclear submarine passed by
his dying place, but also porpoises, gray whales.
Did you know people held parties
on the backs of sea monsters in the 1700s?
These old maps make me wonder
if we could redraw ourselves, who might put a beret
on a tombstone or favorite ocean mammal,
who might grab on to the low-hanging letters
like the gggggggs of a jungle gym—like children
grasping for the next ring, we keep holding on.

THE WORLD OWES ME

nothing. Not the safety
I crave, not the blue skies, the sun
melting anxiety into rivers
of wax, crayons on the driveway,
because I have a driveway,
because I have a car to put in that driveway.
And the world owes me
not much, not happiness, not less
sadness, not a well-fed family
or floating bridge or unpotholed roadway
to my town of barnacles, sea anemones,
one seal barking on a driftwood shore.
I will never be Person of the Year
or Woman of the Decade, I'd just be okay
being someone who didn't muck up
the moment, the environment,
an afternoon with a friend.
I don't need notifications of who
liked my post, how many people found
my review helpful, but give me
a minute of being the hero
to an injured waxwing, the lost
dog, or to hold the sweet sea
of the seabirds when the plastic caps
wash up, a wet god trying to spit out
the seeds. I can't stomach
what the ocean holds in its belly,
and yet so often I walk shorelines with you,
forgetful of how much we have to lose.

What I Call Erosion

Today's sea seems tired of stealing
acres of sand from the beach.

What I call erosion, the waves call:
I wish the wind would stop rushing us,
I wish we could just take it slow.

In the beauty of whitecaps, I sometimes
see sadness, sometimes how lucky we are
to watch the sunrise one more time.

There's so much we're carrying these days—
an osprey clutches a fish in its talons,
a killdeer runs across the dunes
trying to distract us from its nest.

Danger, even when it's not, is everywhere.
Sometimes I pretend to have a broken wing
as I look out the window. But then a cloudscape
in a world of buffleheads, of saltwater roses,

and I forget fear. It's 7 a.m. on a Thursday
and an otter is pretending none of my concerns
matter. The otter, if laughter were a mammal,
dives in and out of the waves, playful.

When the planet says, *This is impossible,*
the otter responds, *Only if you believe it.*

GALA MELANCHOLIA

At the end of the day, a celebration
at the rehab center across the street,
which is what my neighbors call their home
facing west, watching every sunset
as if it's a channel, a show they can't miss.

    In the yard, two mourning doves sit in the grass
    and we conduct a formal meeting about why
    the trees keep leaving. Between wildfires
    and clear-cuts, I have some explaining to do.
    As I talk to the doves, I hear my neighbors toast

another sunset, toast the kingfisher
who screeches by like a party favor,
a fringe squawker, confetti popper.
How easy it is to both love and hate
endings. I turn to tell the doves

    I sometimes wonder if we'll get through this,
    but I'm left with the flap of their wings
    as they rise into a pink sky
    filled with streamers, sparrows,
    and banners of perfectly placed clouds.

We Could Go On Indefinitely Being Swept Off Our Feet

I don't believe in perfection
    or that the metal detector will find
        my lost wedding ring or the silver fish
bracelet I dropped while dancing in a corner
    of a continent where responsibilities
        were tropical drinks, but you could count
yourself a hero, or maybe the luckiest person
    in the world if you made it home safely
        without slicing your foot on the metal
steps to the beach. These days, I believe people
    will fall asleep in moments when we need them
        to be awake for us, and we will be judged
for something we never thought of.
    I trust the thirst we feel is trying to tell us something
        if we listen to it. And people will forget
to wear sunblock and my skin will tire
    and wrinkle, and I'll be so Georgia O'Keeffe about it,
        saying, *Love me for my lines,* for the life
I led because the future is a boiling
    pot of water, the future is a misspelled world.
        Today I cried when I read about a dolphin
caught in a net, something I forget still
    happens, but *hush*—today's storm is not as severe
        as the meteorologists report, and yes, the news
is run by men who look in the mirror
    and make fingerguns at their reflections
        thinking, *This is living, baby,* though maybe
living is watching less TV and trying
    not to fall on a friend's sandcastle.
        It seems we always have our fingers in
each other's dirt. Occasionally, the rain
    stops and the sun becomes a luxury to anyone
        with my zip code, and from my beach chair

I really believe I hear the buzzing
        of someone in another country setting down
                their metal detector and reaching into the sand
to pick up my silver bracelet and diamond ring,
        believing they are the luckiest person on Earth.

Thank You for Saving Me, Someday I'll Save You Too

It's not the flock of advice I love,
but how he said, *You need to get the fuck out of here,*
just before the room went up in flames. Understand
there wasn't water, understand *abandon ship*
means nothing when you're not sinking.
A relationship with fire is all in a day's work—
or that's what he thinks. *It's hard to see the good,*
he said. Our hands on the heart of the planet,
turning the switch to OFF. This is how he saw it
when he couldn't save the world, couldn't save the soul
who stroked out on the roof and fell fifteen feet onto
his neck, or the dark-haired man who looked like his own
reflection—a shadow on the floor in the back
of a church. He tried to joke, *Absinthe makes the heart
grow fonder,* then stayed away an extra day,
the fire station, his second home. But when the tides
kept rising and the fires burned, we learned the best advice
did not come from God or a guidebook,
the best advice sang hopeful from the lost
sparrow on the pine beam, struggling but able
to fly, wingbeats of Morse code: *Follow me into the light*
..-. --- .-.. .-.. --- .-- / -- . / .. -. - --- / - .... . / .-.. .. --. .... -

Notes

Dialogues with Rising Tides takes its name from Galileo's 1616 essay "Discourse on the Tides" and his book *Dialogue Concerning the Two Chief World Systems* (which he referred to as his Dialogue on the Tides). In both documents, he tries to explain the motion of Earth's tides.

Section titles "Cross Rip," "Breaksea," "Scarweather," "Black Deep," "Overfalls," "Shambles," and "Relief" are names of UK & US lightvessels. A lightvessel (or lightship) is "a ship equipped with a brilliant light and moored at a place dangerous to navigation." Lightvessels "are used in waters that are too deep or otherwise unsuitable for lighthouse construction."

"String Theory Relationships" was inspired by Mary Peelen's poem "String Theory."

The last line in "Unsustainable" plays on a quote by Dale Carnegie; the exact quote is "If you want to gather honey, don't kick over the beehive."

"Whiskey-Sour-of-the-Nipple Story" takes its title from a phrase in Anne Sexton's poem "Love Letter Written in a Burning Building."

"Lining Up the Bones" is for Diane Seuss and inspired by her poem "I Have Lived My Whole Life in a Painting Called Paradise."

"Lightvessel" makes reference to two books by Ram Dass, *Be Here Now* and *Cook Book for a Sacred Life.*

"Bravery" is after Catherine Barnett's poem "Son in August."

"To Have and Have Not" takes its title from the Ernest Hemingway novel of the same name. The phrase "the American dream when it becomes a nightmare, their only drawback the mess they leave for relatives to clean up" is from the same book. The phrase "winner take nothing" is also the title of a collection of short stories by Hemingway.

In "Wintercearig Waltz," the word *wintercearig* is from Old English and translates to "winter sorrow" or "winter sadness"; it has been described as "a feeling of a deep sadness, usually comparable to the cold, still, dark heart of full winter."

"Hesitation Waltz": "You know how I always seem to be struggling, even when the situation doesn't call for it?" is a quote from Carrie Fisher's *Postcards from the Edge*.

"Till Death Shatters the Fabulous Stars" takes its title from the last line of Sylvia Plath's poem "Tale of a Tub," and the quote "you are here to be swallowed up" is from the novel *The Painted Drum* by Louise Erdrich.

"The Sun Doesn't Know It's a Star" takes its title from a Madewell sweatshirt.

"Getting an IUD on the Day of 45's Inauguration" is dedicated to Jenn Givhan who told me, "You need to write the poem."

"Facedown" is for Ted Schmid.

"Americanitis" is a term coined by William James about upper-class Americans who "were so familiar with its symptoms (fatigue, anxiety, irritability)" (*New York Times*, April 18, 2017). The image of "guns . . . a belt, and the treasure" was taken from *The Adventures of Tom Sawyer*.

"Unsinkable" is after Ellen Bass's poem "Relax."

"If I Had to Live Again" takes its title from a quote by Mary Ruefle: "If I had my life to live again, I'd be a poet." Theodore Roethke died in a Bainbridge Island swimming pool, which has now been converted into a Zen garden at the Bloedel Reserve.

The poem title "We Could Go On Indefinitely Being Swept Off Our Feet" is a nod to Zelda Fitzgerald and her book *Save Me the Waltz*. The actual quote: "We couldn't go on indefinitely being swept off our feet."

"Thank You for Saving Me, Someday I'll Save You Too": The title of this poem was inspired by a quote from Zelda Fitzgerald: "Thanks again for saving me. Someday, I'll save you too." "..-. --- .-.. .-.. --- .-- / -- . / .. -. - --- / - ..... / .-.. .. --. .... -" is Morse code for "follow me into the light."

About the Author

Kelli Russell Agodon is the cofounder of Two Sylvias Press as well as the codirector of Poets on the Coast: A Weekend Writing Retreat for Women. She has been guest faculty and a guest speaker for several universities and MFA programs. Agodon lives in a sleepy seaside town in Washington State and is an avid paddleboarder and hiker. You can write to her directly at kelli@agodon.com or visit her website: www.agodon.com. *Dialogues with Rising Tides* is her fourth collection of poems.

Poetry is vital to language and living. Since 1972, Copper Canyon Press has published extraordinary poetry from around the world to engage the imaginations and intellects of readers, writers, booksellers, librarians, teachers, students, and donors.

Copper Canyon Press gratefully acknowledges the kindness, patronage, and generous support of Jean Marie Lee, whose love and passionate appreciation of poetry has provided an everlasting benefit to our publishing program.

WE ARE GRATEFUL FOR THE MAJOR SUPPORT PROVIDED BY:

THE PAUL G. ALLEN FAMILY FOUNDATION

TO LEARN MORE ABOUT UNDERWRITING
COPPER CANYON PRESS TITLES,
PLEASE CALL 360-385-4925 EXT. 103

WE ARE GRATEFUL FOR THE MAJOR SUPPORT PROVIDED BY:

Anonymous

Jill Baker and Jeffrey Bishop

Anne and Geoffrey Barker

In honor of Ida Bauer, Betsy Gifford, and Beverly Sachar

Donna and Matthew Bellew

Will Blythe

John Branch

Diana Broze

John R. Cahill

Sarah Cavanaugh

The Beatrice R. and Joseph A. Coleman Foundation

The Currie Family Fund

Stephanie Ellis-Smith and Douglas Smith

Laurie and Oskar Eustis

Austin Evans

Saramel Evans

Mimi Gardner Gates

Gull Industries Inc. on behalf of William True

The Trust of Warren A. Gummow

William R. Hearst, III

Carolyn and Robert Hedin

Bruce Kahn

Phil Kovacevich and Eric Wechsler

Lakeside Industries Inc. on behalf of Jeanne Marie Lee

Maureen Lee and Mark Busto

Peter Lewis and Johnna Turiano

Ellie Mathews and Carl Youngmann as The North Press

Larry Mawby and Lois Bahle

Hank and Liesel Meijer

Jack Nicholson

Gregg Orr

Petunia Charitable Fund and adviser Elizabeth Hebert

Gay Phinny

Suzanne Rapp and Mark Hamilton

Adam and Lynn Rauch

Emily and Dan Raymond

Jill and Bill Ruckelshaus

Cynthia Sears

Kim and Jeff Seely

Joan F. Woods

Barbara and Charles Wright

Caleb Young as C. Young Creative

The dedicated interns and faithful volunteers of Copper Canyon Press